On West Highland Lines

Robert Robotham

First published 1997

ISBN 0 7110 2526 6

Published by Ian Allan Publishing

an imprint of Ian Allan Ltd, Terminal House, Station Approach, Shepperton, Surrey TW17 8AS. Printed by Ian Allan Printing Ltd at its works at Coombelands in Runnymede, England.

Code: 9705/C2

Right:
'Black 5' No 44996 makes a fine sight as she thrashes up to Tyndrum with the 12 noon from Mallaig to Glasgow Queen Street in September 1959. The line ran along the side of the mountain to obviate the need for a long viaduct across the valley floor. *SC850 Colour-Rail*

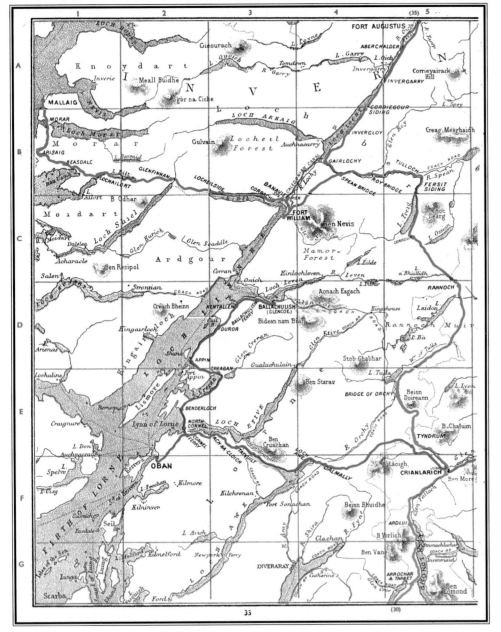

Front cover:
A stiff climb of roughly three miles at 1:50 awaited trains out of Oban that inevitably meant the double-heading of heavier services. A classic view of Oban is seen here as Standard Class '4MT' 2-6-0 No 76001 and 'Black 5' 4-6-0 No 45115 wait to depart from Oban station with a return Television Excursion train to Glasgow on 20 May 1960. The television train ran from Glasgow Buchanan Street via Callander to Oban, then returned to Glasgow Queen Street via the West Highland. The train was equipped with a TV studio and monitors in the carriages that allowed passengers to entertain their fellow travellers! It was also used by schools for educational purposes.
Mike Mensing

Back cover:
The rugged nature of the terrain that the West Highland lines had to negotiate is well illustrated as BRCW Bo-Bo diesel D5359 passes the eastern end of Loch Eilt with the 3.5pm Mallaig to Fort William on 13 July 1965. *Mike Mensing*

Left:
Map from showing the two West Highland lines from Crianlarich: the Callander & Oban (red) and the West Highland (blue), taken from the *British Railways Atlas 1947. Ian Allan Ltd*

Introduction

This book focuses on two railways that make up the West Highland lines — namely the former West Highland Railway from Glasgow Queen Street to Fort William and Mallaig and the Callander & Oban line from Dunblane to Oban. The aim is to illustrate, through colour pictures, the routes in the 1950s and 1960s when a variety of pre-Grouping and more modern forms of steam traction and early diesels still ran.

For a more detailed account of the lines, *The West Highland Railway* and *The Callander & Oban Railway* by John Thomas, and O. S. Nock's *The Caledonian Railway* make excellent reading. Neil Caplan's *The West Highland Lines*, a *Railway World* Special, is also an authoritative work, as is *The Callander & Oban Railway* by C. E. J. Fryer, published by Oakwood Press.

Thanks are due to Ron White of Colour-Rail and to Mike Mensing, who must rank as one of the highest quality railway photographers of all time. Also, thanks are due to Colin Stewart of Inverness for general help and advice

Robert Robotham
Charlbury
January 1997

Callander to Oban — Background and Construction

The first of the West Highland lines to be built was the Callander & Oban — the aim being to link the Caledonian with the west coast steamers at Oban and prevent the North British getting to the west coast from Glasgow. The 71 miles it had to negotiate were tough and circuitous, climbing from Callander through Strathyre and Balquhidder at 1:56 and then five miles of 1:60 to Glenoglehead at 941ft above sea level. Building work took a long time — eight years to get to Tyndrum from where the line dropped down to Dalmally at 1:55 through Glenlochy. From

Dalmally it passed by Loch Awe and through the Pass of Brander, where there were continual threats of landslides. Oban was reached following switchback gradients culminating with a climb over Glencruitten at 301ft above sea level, with 1:50 approaches in both directions. The Tyndrum to Oban section was 37 miles in length but took only seven years to build as opposed to the aforementioned Callander to Tyndrum's eight years for 34 miles.

The West Highland Railway — Background and Construction

In 1882 a project was launched to build a railway from Glasgow to Inverness via Fort William. The promoters were wary of costs, having seen the experience of the Callander & Oban and considering the difficult terrain the line would have to pass through. The Highland and the Caledonian found this most alarming as they already ran a route to Inverness. They fought the Bill and succeeded in getting the route stopped altogether. Another scheme was submitted in 1889, under the name of the West Highland Railway Co, but on this occasion it ran to Fort William only and not Inverness. The North British was the main sponsor and it intended to operate the line with its own motive power and rolling stock. The Bill was opposed again by the Caledonian and the Highland but on this occasion it passed. Fort William was finally reached on 7 August 1894.

The route from Craigendoran Junction was constructed over difficult terrain, climbing through Helensburgh at 1:58 and then to Rhu at 1:67. From Garelochhead a climb of 1:54 in places over Glen Douglas saw the 1:57 drop to Arrochar & Tarbet. Undulating on to Ardlui, another summit was then climbed up through Crianlarich to Tyndrum, where the line ran on the opposite side of the valley to the Callander & Oban. Much of this was as steep as 1:60, dropping at 1:55 through Bridge of Orchy and then up to Gorton at 1:66. The line runs on over Rannoch Moor to Corrour where for the 28 miles

to Fort William there was a descent of the same severity. Coupled with these steep grades were many tight reverse curves which made working heavy trains difficult and required double-heading of most.

Fort William to Mallaig — Background and Construction

The Fort William to Mallaig section looks less challenging on paper, indeed the first section from Mallaig Junction was virtually level, but after passing Locheilside the climb began through Glenfinnan at up to 1:45, then, once over the summit, dropped through 1:48 to Lochailort. From there the line undulated with many short inclines of up to 1:48, finally dropping into Mallaig at 1:75. Many curves also provided train crews with difficult conditions, it being difficult to get a good run at any of the banks. The original plan for an extension to Roshven was dropped and Mallaig was chosen instead due to pressure from the Admiralty who contributed a grant of £30,000 for the harbour at Mallaig. The line opened on 1 April 1901.

Passenger Services: Callander & Oban

In the 1950s and 1960s the Callander & Oban lines were suffering from the development of road transport. By the late 1950s there were three through trains to and from Edinburgh and Glasgow. A sleeper ran on Fridays from London and back on the Monday. The early 1960s saw four through services to and from Glasgow Buchanan Street via Callander with through carriages for Edinburgh Waverley. One of these services carried an observation car at the rear. There was also a DMU service that combined at Crianlarich with a portion from Fort William for Glasgow Queen Street. Branch services to Killin from the Junction were limited to four return services per day, as was the Connel Ferry to Ballachulish line with three trains running to and from Oban. Between Callander and Dunblane, through trains were supplemented by a local service.

Passenger Services: Glasgow to Fort William and Mallaig

In the 1960s there were through services from Glasgow Queen Street to Fort William supplemented by the King's Cross sleeper. In summer, one of the through trains split with an Oban service at Crianlarich — a DMU in the 1960s — and another carried an observation car.

The Fort William to Mallaig service had six trains per day, — three of these conveying through carriages to and from Glasgow. At the southern end of the route was a local service as far as Arrochar & Tarbet.

Freight Services

The Callander & Oban line saw freight trains of general merchandise and coal, as well as fish sent in insulated containers and wagons. General merchandise and fuel oils were also transhipped for local use and for the Scottish islands.

The Fort William and Mallaig line carried fish and other general traffic to and from the islands. Coastal shipping had a good slice of the freight traffic and the railway found it difficult to make inroads into this market. The first heavy industry came in the mid-1920s with the construction of an aluminium smelter at Fort William. The associated hydroelectric scheme at Lochaber also benefited the railway, as did the outflow of associated aluminium products to the rest of the country and the incoming raw materials from Fife and Blyth. The development of a pulp and paper mill at Corpach has also helped to secure the line's future. Wood pulp traffic from other forwarding points to other paper mills in Scotland has also grown. Oil traffic between Grangemouth and Fort William was also generated by West Highland Oils, and the MoD has stimulated traffic with the naval bases on the Clyde and at Corpach.

Special and Excursion Trains

Summer excursions ran from Glasgow and Edinburgh and in most cases were heavy trains that required double-heading — traditionally by a pair of 'Glens' — especially before the introduction of the more powerful 'K' classes. However, even these were often not powerful enough to handle some trains on their own, and double-heading of 'Black 5s', 'Standard 5s' and 'B1s' was not uncommon. In the 1930s the celebrated 'Northern Belle' from London ran on the West Highland, combining rail travel with a cruise on Loch Lomond. Other services ran timed to connect with the steamers from various departure points and circular tours — out via Callander and back through Craigendoran.

A celebrated working was the 'Six Lochs Land Cruise' — a DMU set that ran a circular tour from Buchanan Street to Queen Street. A six-car DMU that split at Crianlarich ran in the summer and allowed a visit to both Fort William and Oban. Passengers were transferred by steamer and rejoined the DMU sets that then connected at Crianlarich for the run south.

The Amateur Photographers' Excursion train ran on 25 May 1957, complete with slow running to allow good quality photographs to be taken. An exhibition was held in Glasgow Central station of the results. The Scottish Region train that was fitted with its own TV studio and TV monitors also visited and volunteers were invited into the studio to entertain their fellow passengers! The train was also used for educational purposes and was chartered by schools.

As well as specials, most service trains were strengthened in the summer and conveyed through coaches for wider destinations.

Dieselisation

The advent of more modern motive power on the Oban line came in 1961 in the shape of the North British-built Bo-Bo Type 2 locomotives that usually operated in pairs. DMUs also came into service on the local services to Callander from Dunblane and for excursion traffic. The BRCW Bo-Bo Type 2s gradually supplemented and replaced the North British locomotives, surviving until comparatively recently when the Sprinter and Class 37 era arrived. Dieselisation began on the West Highland in 1963 with the ubiquitous Class 27. Class 20s also worked some of the freight services, especially the pulp trains.

Rationalisation

The Reshaping Report published in 1963 indicated a rationalisation in the working of the two lines — recommending closure of the Crianlarich Lower through Callander to Dunblane section, with the rest of the Oban line being served via the West Highland line from Glasgow Queen Street and the 1897 spur at Crianlarich. This spur had been used in the past, but mainly by excursion trains and some regular services which started on 23 May 1949. The line through to Callander closed on 27 September 1965 — early, due to a rock-fall — the spur from Dunblane to Callander being retained until the official closure date of 1 November 1965. The Killin Junction to Killin line closed in September 1965 along with the main line and the Connel Ferry to Ballachulish route on 23 March 1966. Balquhidder to Comrie had closed long before this date, in October 1951.

This book now goes on to illustrate the train services on the West Highland routes in the 1950s and and 1960s — when steam was still supreme — but with an influx of diesel power.

Right:
'Black 5s' were common performers on the Callander & Oban section. Here, No 44798 arrives at Callander with a train from Oban to Glasgow in July 1958. Originally the footbridge at Callander was an ornate affair, complete with a clock, but this was destroyed in an accident in 1947 when a runaway freight train collided with a passenger train in the station. Thankfully no one was hurt. *The late W. Oliver/SC137 Colour-Rail*

The Callander & Oban
Callander to Killin Junction

Above:
A real 'old-timer' in the shape of Drummond 'Standard Goods' No 57324 of 1883 vintage stands at Callander on 24 July 1958. The 'Standard Goods' were classified '2F' and worked a variety of freight and local passenger turns as well as being used on the branch to Killin. In former days they also acted as pilot locomotives for double-heading heavy passenger trains. Callander station has now been demolished, making way for a car park as with so many other railway stations. *Colour-Rail*

Right:
The BR Standard Class 4MT 2-6-4 tank locomotives were common visitors and replaced the older Caledonian and LMS types as they in turn were replaced by diesels in other parts of Scotland. No 80126 of Perth shed is seen shunting empty coaching stock of the 2.40pm Killin to Callander on 4 May 1965 — only a few months before closure in the autumn of that year. Callander became famous as Tannochbrae in the original 1960s TV series *Dr Finlay's Casebook. J. M. Boyes/Colour-Rail*

Above:
'Black 5' No 44724 is seen with an Oban to Glasgow service approaching Balquhidder on 27 July 1957. Balquhidder was the junction of the line to Comrie and Crieff and then on to Perth. This line was partially closed — from Comrie to Lochearnhead — in October 1951, thus depriving Balquhidder of junction status. Note the immaculate permanent way maintenance provided by the gangers from Craig-na-Cailleach which regularly won awards for the 'Prize Length'. No weeds in those days! Balquhidder station was once used as a church for the local inhabitants.
Colour-Rail

Right:
Climbing the 1:60 to Glenoglehead Summit are two North British Locomotive Co diesels, D6102 and D6123, with the 12 noon from Glasgow Buchanan Street and 11.40am from Edinburgh Princes Street to Oban. The NBL Bo-Bos were regular performers in the early 1960s, this scene being taken on 17 May 1961. At Glenoglehead was a passing loop and originally this was the station for Killin until the branch opened in 1886. A rock-fall near Glenoglehead closed the line prematurely in September 1965 — weeks in advance of the proposed closure date.
Mike Mensing

Killin Junction to Killin

Below:
'2P' 0-4-4 tank No 55263 of Oban/Ballachulish shed waits at Killin Junction with the single coach of the 2.46pm to Killin on 16 May 1960. The branch was dominated by steam traction right through to the end — only DMUs on the 'Six Loch Land Cruise' trains in the early 1960s making any impression. No 55263 was a post-Grouping development of the Caledonian '439' standard passenger class of tank locomotives designed by McIntosh and introduced in 1925.
Mike Mensing

Left:
In appalling weather conditions, Caledonian Single No 123 and two BRCW Bo-Bo diesel locomotives meet at Killin Junction on 11 April 1963. No 123 was working an SLS Special, the 'Scottish Rambler', an Easter tour of the Callander & Oban. A year before, on 12 May 1962, No 123 worked a special from Glasgow to Oban and back with NBR 'Glen' No 256 *Glen Douglas. K. M. Falconer/ P285 Colour-Rail*

Above:
'Black 5' No 45125 arrives at Killin Junction with a service for Oban on 18 June 1960. Note the gradient post showing a descent of 1:60. The branch to Killin and Loch Tay curves away to the left. Behind the locomotive is a 12-wheeler dining car, regularly included in formations on the Oban run.
Colour-Rail

Above:
BR '4MT' No 80126 heads towards Killin Junction with the 9.56am from Killin on a glorious day — 14 August 1962. Trains on the branch were often mixed.
Colour-Rail

Right:
In June 1965, a single coach and BR '4MT' No 80028 storm off to Killin Junction and cross the superb viaduct, seemingly attracting little interest from the lady enjoying the sound of the water on the Dochart!
SC854 Colour-Rail

Right:
'Black 5s' No 44881 and an unidentified sister get away from Crianlarich Lower with a service from Oban to Glasgow and Edinburgh on 22 May 1961. After the closure of the Callander & Oban route east of Crianlarich in autumn 1965 the station area survived as a wood-pulp loading point for traffic from there to Corpach paper mill. The station yard survived until the early 1990s. *The late John McCann/SC934 Colour-Rail*

Above:
No 55204 is seen on 17 May 1961 at Killin station, having arrived with the 11.27am from Killin Junction. No 52204 had just been down to Loch Tay to take on water and coal, leaving the coach in the platform. To run round the train at Killin the locomotive would move into the siding, leaving the coach in the platform. The guard would then let off the brake, the coach would run past the locomotive using gravity as propulsion and then the engine would 'hook on' to take the train back to the junction at 1.42pm. *Mike Mensing*

Right:
The Killin Junction to Killin and Loch Tay Pier line opened in 1886, where before World War 1 connections were made with sailings on the loch. In September 1939 the line between Loch Tay and Killin closed, but locomotives did travel there to be serviced at the small shed. Standard '4' No 80126 is watered at Loch Tay on 3 May 1965 as it waits for the climb up to Killin Junction with another branch service. At this time the station building at Loch Tay was used as a private house. *J. M. Boyes/Colour-Rail*

Above:
Crianlarich West Junction is seen in June 1965. Standard '4MT' No 80028 heads two vans up to the junction to shunt them back into the sidings at the Lower. The connection between the West Highland and Callander & Oban lines is seen on the right. It first started regular services from Glasgow Queen Street on 23 May 1949. In the background, the West Highland line viaduct can be seen taking the line from Glasgow on to Tyndrum Upper and Fort William. *SC853 Colour-Rail*

Right:
'Black 5s' Nos 44925 and 45013 storm up the 1:71/1:62 to Tyndrum Lower with the 12 noon Glasgow to Oban on 12 September 1959. Between Tyndrum and Dalmally was a loop at Glenlochy Crossing controlled by a combined house and signalbox. *Colour-Rail*

Above:
'Black 5' No 45049 and 'B1' No 61278 approach Loch Awe with the 12.5pm Oban to Glasgow and Edinburgh on 15 May 1961. The train is travelling under the eastern slopes of Ben Cruachan. *Mike Mensing*

Right:
NBL Bo-Bo diesels D6108 and D6135 run through the Pass of Brander with the 12 noon from Glasgow Buchanan Street to Oban on 13 May 1961. The line through the pass is protected against rock-falls by a wire safety fence, first installed on the instruction of the Callander & Oban's secretary, John Anderson. The winds in the pass caused this to vibrate making a musical noise and earning it the name of 'Anderson's Piano'. Should the fence break due to a rock-fall, the signals automatically return to danger. *Mike Mensing*

Left:
'Black 5' No 45159 leaves Taynuilt station with the short 9.30am Oban to Glasgow on 17 May 1960. *Mike Mensing*

Right:
DMUs were used on the Oban line on excursion trains and here a train from Glasgow to Oban arrives at Taynuilt on 17 May 1960. The unit is a Swindon-built Cross-Country set and is well loaded with day trippers from the central belt of Scotland. This was the Oban portion of the DMU that split at Crianlarich with Oban and Fort William day trippers who were to enjoy a steamer trip between the two ports before returning to Glasgow. *Mike Mensing*

Above:
Ex-Caledonian '3F' '652' class 0-6-0 No 57635 of 1899 stands in Connel Ferry station before leaving for Oban on 15 May 1961. No 57635 had been to Ballachulish with a pick-up freight and this was the return working. The train had to run round at Connel Ferry as the direct spur planned to serve Oban was never completed. *Mike Mensing*

Right:
15 May 1961 also saw 'Black 5' No 45048 leaving Connel Ferry station with a Glasgow-bound freight. An impressive Caledonian signal shows the road clear to Taynuilt. *Mike Mensing*

Connel Ferry to Ballachulish

Above:
Ex-LMS 2-6-0 No 46460 passes over the impressive Connel Ferry rail/road bridge
with a service to Ballachulish in April 1962. A classic motorcycle and Ford Popular
wait for the train to cross. The bridge carried the railway and road over Loch Etive
and survives today, although only for road traffic. It has a span of 500ft and is
designed on the cantilever principle — as is the Forth Bridge. These Ivatt locomotives
were brought into service on the branch for a short period in the early 1960s to cover
the period between the withdrawal of the 0-4-4 tanks and the introduction of the
BRCW diesels. *Colour-Rail*

Right:
The first station on the branch was North Connel and on 18 May 1961 ex-LMS '2P'
0-4-4 tank No 55263 calls with the 10.48am from Ballachulish to Connel Ferry.
Mike Mensing

Below:
McIntosh 0-4-4 tank No 55124, dating from 1895, heads for Connel Ferry and Oban with a service from Ballachulish in May 1961. The line is seen skirting Loch Leven and passengers had wonderful views of the surrounding area. No 55124 was a '19' class locomotive with a railed coal bunker.
SC614 Colour-Rail

Left:
Drummond Caledonian 'Standard Goods' No 57276 stands with a ballast train for the P-way gangers near Kentallen on the Ballachulish line in May 1957. The train is seen by the shore of Loch Linnhe.
SC147 Colour-Rail

Above:
In the last years of operation of the branch, diesels had established themselves as the main type of motive power in the area (having been introduced from 1962), the BRCW classes proving more reliable than the NBL types. BRCW Bo-Bo D5363 calls at Ballachulish Ferry with the 12.35pm Connel Ferry to Ballachulish on 15 July 1965. The station was situated next to the ferry across Loch Leven which has now been replaced by a bridge. *Mike Mensing*

Below:
A contrast with the 1957 photograph shows D5357 with a service for Connel Ferry on 14 August 1962. The locomotive and coaches are in immaculate condition and a new Mk 1 coach has found its way into the ex-LNER set. The station is impressively situated with the Pap of Glencoe dominating the scene in the background. *Colour-Rail*

Above:
LMS 0-4-4 tank No 55263 stands in the terminus station at Ballachulish with a Connel Ferry service on 27 July 1957. These locomotives were the main type of power used on the branch, with other ex-Caledonian varieties, until the advent of the Ivatt Moguls and, latterly, dieselisation. There was also a small goods yard to the side of the station served by a pick-up freight service from Oban. *Colour-Rail*

Connel Ferry to Oban

'Black 5' No 45423 leaves Connel Ferry with the 6.50am from Edinburgh Princes Street/7.50am Glasgow Buchanan Street to Oban on 18 May 1961. The 'Black 5' faced a climb as steep as 1:50 up to Glencruitten Crossing before the sharp descent into Oban. In the background a bridge on the never completed direct spur from Oban to Ballachulish is clearly seen. *Mike Mensing*

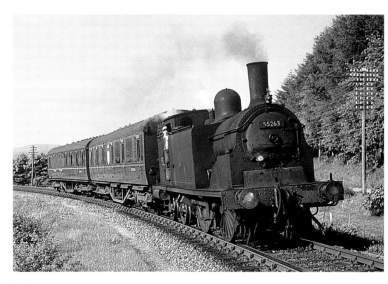

Left:
The gradient is well illustrated as the evening sun catches 'Black 5' No 45396 climbing the 1:50 up to Glencruitten Crossing (301ft above sea level) with a freight for Oban on 18 May 1961. *Mike Mensing*

Above:
Most services from Ballachulish ran through to Oban and '2P' No 55263 heads through Glencruitten with the 8.25am from Oban to Ballachulish in May 1961. However, the midday branch service laid over at Connel Ferry and connected with express services to and from Oban. *Mike Mensing/Colour-Rail*

Right:
Originally, the section from Connel Ferry to Oban was six miles of single line, but such was the increase in traffic that a loop was opened at Glencruitten on 9 October 1901. Ex-Caledonian '2P' tank No 55224 makes a spectacular climb up the 1:50 out of Oban with the 4.55pm Oban to Ballachulish on 21 May 1960 and is approaching Glencruitten Crossing. The driver has the tablet for the single-line section from Oban ready to hand in. The signalbox, visible towards the front of the train, was a large Gothic-style house with the actual lever frame in a room overlooking the line. The loop has not survived today, closing in May 1966. *Mike Mensing*

Above:
Another Ballachulish service — this time the 3.57pm to Oban — arrives at Glencruitten Crossing to pass the 5.15pm Oban to Glasgow and Edinburgh. '2P' No 55238 is in charge and the date is 21 May 1960. No 55238 was introduced in 1922 — a Pickersgill '431' class locomotive developed from the McIntosh design, with a special cast-iron front buffer beam for banking. *Mike Mensing*

Right:
Dropping down into Oban with a short freight comes 'Black 5' No 45396 on 16 May 1961 at 8.18pm. *Mike Mensing*

Left:
Oban station pilot '2MT' 2-6-0 No 46468 is seen at Oban Goods Junction shunting petrol tankers back into Oban petrol sidings in May 1962. The drop in the 1:50 gradient can be clearly seen behind the train. The Ivatt Mogul was brought into the area to work the Ballachulish branch after the '2P' tanks were withdrawn.
SC667 Colour-Rail

Above:
An excellent overall view of Oban Yard sees ex-Caledonian '3F' 0-6-0 No 57635 arriving with the return pick-up freight from Ballachulish on 18 May 1961 at 4.15pm.
Mike Mensing

Right:
A photograph that says it all about the Caledonian at Oban. Ex-Caledonian '2P' tank No 55238 waits with the immaculate empty stock of a train from Glasgow and Edinburgh on 20 May 1960. A rake of equally immaculate Gresley coaches stand in the next platform. Some fine delivery lorries wait on the left platform. These platforms, which were outside the station buildings, were built during 1903 on the opening of the Ballachulish line. Oban is a gateway to the Western Islands, and freight, including petrol and oil, was transferred from rail to and from the ships here. *Mike Mensing*

Above:
Standard Class 5 4-6-0s supplemented the 'Black 5s' on the Oban route and here No 73151 brews up nicely as she awaits departure with a Glasgow and Edinburgh service in May 1960. No 73151 was fitted with Capprotti valve gear which is well illustrated in this photograph. Petrol wagons can be seen in the sidings to the right of the locomotive. *Colour-Rail*

Right:
New meets not quite so new at Oban! Two NBL diesels, Nos D6135 and D6108, wait to leave Oban with the 5.15pm to Glasgow Buchanan Street and Edinburgh Princes Street on 13 May 1961. 'Black 5' No 44881 looks on with the empty stock of the 12 noon from Glasgow and Edinburgh. The NBL types did not prove as successful as the BRCW locomotives and were gradually replaced. *Mike Mensing*

The West Highland
Craigendoran Junction to Fort William

Left:
The West Highland route started at Craigendoran Junction and climbed almost immediately up to Helensburgh Upper. On 11 April 1959, Reid North British 'C15' tank locomotive No 67460 propels a local service to Arrochar & Tarbet past the junction box.
W. P. de Beer/Colour-Rail

Below:
The first station was Craigendoran itself and 'C15' 4-4-2 tank No 67474 waits with the push-pull service to Arrochar & Tarbet. The Reid 4-4-2 tanks gave sterling service on the route and dated from 1911. With her sisters Nos 67475 and 67460 in the previous photograph, they were fitted for push-pull operation and based at Eastfield shed.
SC780 Colour-Rail

Below:
'C15' No 67474 is seen again, but this time at Shandon
with a train for Glasgow in 1958. Note the express
headlamps on what is a 'local' service — these were
carried by all West Highland
passenger trains. *Colour-Rail*

Above:
After Helensburgh Upper came Rhu and Shandon followed by Garelochhead. 'C15' No 67460 arrives at Garelochhead with the local service in May 1959. This local service was withdrawn on 14 June 1964, but over 30 years later an early morning local service from Garelochhead to Glasgow has been reintroduced in autumn 1996. *SC385 Colour-Rail*

Right:
The climb through Garelochhead saw a steep rise of as much as 1:54 in places up to the summit at Glen Douglas where there was a passing place and siding. A Fort William train is double-headed up through Garelochhead by 'Black 5' No 44973 and 'B1' No 61243 *Sir Harold Mitchell* on 1 September 1959. *Colour-Rail*

Left:
Arrochar & Tarbet was a crossing point and two BRCW diesels, Nos D5359 and
D5361, arrive with a train for Fort William and prepare to cross a Glasgow-bound
service. The second man has the tablet ready — he was lucky he was not shovelling
coal into a hungry steam locomotive! The date is 31 May 1963. *Colour-Rail*

Above:
The local service from Glasgow and Craigendoran terminated at Arrochar & Tarbet.
'C15' No 67460, in immaculate condition, is posed with two children in June 1958.
Good detail of the push-pull equipment is seen on the locomotive.
SC505 Colour-Rail

Below:
'Black 5s' No 44968 and an unidentified sister get away from Crianlarich Upper with a Glasgow service in June 1962. Crianlarich Upper also had a turntable and shed which was used to store withdrawn GC-type 'D11' 'Scottish Directors' in the 1960s and is still used by the engineers' department.
C. G. Harrison/Colour-Rail

Left:
Trains also crossed at Ardlui, the start of a steep climb through Crianlarich to Tyndrum. 'Black 5s' Nos 44967 and 44956 on a Mallaig and Fort William to Glasgow Queen Street train cross classmate No 44968 with a Glasgow to Fort William service on 10 September 1959. *The late Malcolm Thompson/ Colour-Rail*

Above:
At Crianlarich the West Highland crossed over the Callander & Oban. There was also a link between the two routes that dated from 20 December 1897. Some services ran through from Glasgow Queen Street onto the Oban line; these started regularly from 23 May 1949. 'B1' No 61336 takes a freight train for Fort William over the viaduct from Crianlarich Upper to Tyndrum and on to Fort William in August 1948.
SC638 Colour-Rail

Above:
The traditional motive power on West Highland passenger trains were the North British 'Glen' class 'D34' 4-4-0s. Nos 62496 *Glen Loy* and 62471 *Glen Falloch* are seen crossing a Glasgow-bound freight train at Crianlarich Upper on 9 May 1959. The 'Glens' are heading the 5.45am Glasgow Queen Street to Fort William, a train that conveyed sleeping cars from London King's Cross. By this time the 'Glens' had been replaced by other power, starting with the 'K2s' in the 1930s, but were used on this occasion in connection with the filming of the TV programme *Railway Roundabout. Colour-Rail*

Right:
'Standard 5' No 73077 and 'B1' No 61243 *Sir Harold Mitchell* are dwarfed by the magnificence of Ben Doran as they double-head the 1pm Mallaig to Glasgow at Tyndrum on 12 September 1959. The railway at this point runs along the side of the valley in a series of sweeping curves, the largest of which is known as Horse Shoe Curve. *Colour-Rail*

47

Above:
'Black 5' No 44957 has a permanent way train in Tyndrum Upper station on 19 May 1960. The 'Black 5s' soon infiltrated the West Highland line after Nationalisation in 1948, proving as successful as the LNER designs that had been previously dominant. *Mike Mensing*

Right:
Gorton Crossing provided a passing loop between Bridge of Orchy and Rannoch and was one of the remotest stations in Britain. It could be switched out as required, but as a result did not provide much of a career for railway staff. This, coupled with its location, made it difficult to recruit anyone to work there. Amazingly, an old coach body was placed on the platform to act as a school for local children. 'Glens' Nos 62496 *Glen Loy* and 62471 *Glen Falloch* wait in the loop with the 5.45am Glasgow Queen Street to Mallaig on 9 September 1959. This area of the line was particularly susceptible to bad weather, Gorton being covered completely by snow in January 1963. The loop is still used for engineers' trains. *Colour-Rail*

Above:
From the footplate of 'Glen' 62496 *Glen Loy* on 9 September 1959 at Rannoch station a clear road ahead is seen complete with the station staff and tablet for the section to Corrour. The memorial on the platform is to J. H. Renton who, as one of the directors of the West Highland, gave much of his personal fortune to allow construction of the line to continue, following a period of financial hardship. As a result, the navvies produced a fine figurehead portrait carving which still stands to this day. *Colour-Rail*

Right:
'Standard 5' No 73078 and 'Black 5' No 44956 leave Rannoch and pass over the spectacular 684ft-long viaduct with the 7.30pm ex-King's Cross (previous night) 5.45am from Glasgow Queen Street to Mallaig on 20 May 1961. The sleeper still runs today — but only after a fight! Construction problems with the trackbed foundations in the Rannoch area caused engineers to use rafts of brushwood as a base, the method adopted by George Stephenson's Liverpool & Manchester Railway at Chat Moss. *Mike Mensing*

Above:
English Electric 1,000hp Bo-Bo locomotive, now Class 20, D8095 heads a very mixed Fort William-bound freight past the north of Loch Treig on 16 July 1965. *Mike Mensing*

Right:
The two 'Glens', Nos 62496 and 62471, on the 5.45am from King's Cross and Glasgow Queen Street to Mallaig are seen again, this time waiting at Tulloch on 9 September 1959. The home depot of Eastfield is painted on the buffer beam of the leading locomotive. *Colour-Rail*

Left:
More modern motive power in the shape of BRCW Bo-Bo D5361 heads the 7.48am Mallaig to Glasgow Queen Street one mile south of Tulloch on 5 July 1965. The climb to the summit, just to the north of Corrour (1,350ft) was mostly at 1:57 from Spean Bridge — a distance of some 19 miles. *Mike Mensing*

Above:
The BRCW locomotives did not totally monopolise West Highland services and this is illustrated by NBL Bo-Bo D6103 heading a Glasgow service through the Monessie Gorge in April 1968. The gorge was carved out by the River Spean and the line runs on a ledge, carved into the wall of the gorge. Note the blue/grey coach adding a touch of colour as well as the yellow warning paint on the front of the locomotive.
The late Derek Cross/Colour-Rail

SPEAN BRIDGE
CHANGE FOR
INVERGARRY AND FORT
AUGUSTUS BUS SERVICE

Left:
Spean Bridge was once the junction for the Invergarry & Fort Augustus Railway — an independent line that opened in 1903 and ran up the Great Glen to Fort Augustus at the southern tip of Loch Ness. Unfortunately, it was not successful and closed for passengers as early as 1 December 1933 and to freight on 1 January 1947. BRCW diesel D5368 arrives with the 7.48am Mallaig to Glasgow on 6 July 1965. The station sign offers a bus service, instead of the long-closed railway, for Invergarry and Fort Augustus. *Mike Mensing*

Above:
BRCW diesel D5368 leaves Spean Bridge with the 7.48am Mallaig to Glasgow Queen Street on 6 July 1965. *Mike Mensing*

Left:
A powerful LNER combination of 'K1' No 62034 and 'B1' No 61342 leaves the Mallaig line, east of Fort William, with the 1pm from Mallaig to Glasgow Queen Street on 20 May 1961. Note the line in the background, on the bridge, which was the 3ft narrow gauge railway built to serve the local aluminium smelter. It stretched from Loch Linnhe to Loch Treig. *Mike Mensing*

Above:
BR did experiment with other motive power for the West Highland route — but the 'Clans' did not perform on the line which makes this scene all the more rare. No 72001 *Clan Cameron* stands at Fort William station on 16 June 1956 with the stock of the special train that ran in connection with the gathering of the Clan Cameron at Achnacarry. The train ran from Glasgow to Spean Bridge and a rehearsal of the run was made on 10 May when No 72001 hauled the 3.46pm from Glasgow to Fort William and returned the following day with the 9.31am. Fittingly, the crew working the special all had the surname of Cameron. The railway authorities were suspicious of the Class 6 Pacific and 'K4' *Cameron of Locheil* was based at Crianlarich as a standby. *K. Bannister/SC931 Colour-Rail*

Below:
'Black 5' 44908 arrives at Fort William with a service from Glasgow on 28 September 1959. The station nameboard proudly advises passengers to change for Kinlochleven, Glencoe and Ballachulish — the latter destination also being accessible by the alternative Callander & Oban route. *SC935 Colour-Rail*

Right:
A classic scene of Fort William station in August 1959 complete with its battlements, with 'K2' No 61787 *Loch Quoich* having arrived from Glasgow. The local road transport is in evidence waiting for parcels and mails off the train. No 61787 was a Gresley design and a 'K2/2' variant introduced in 1914 with a side window cab. The proximity of the original Fort William station to the harbour is evident, along with the suitable clothing of the passengers who look well equipped to deal with the Scottish weather. *SC326 Colour-Rail*

Above:
On 30 July 1958, 'J36' 0-6-0 No 65313 stands at Fort William with the empty stock of an arrival from Mallaig. This station, built to link conveniently with steamers to the Scottish Islands, has now closed and been relocated further east — all due to yet another road improvement scheme. No 65313 was introduced in 1888 and was designed by Matthew Holmes of the North British Railway as a Class C locomotive. She carries the 65J shed code for Fort William/Mallaig. *Colour-Rail*

Above:
Two 'Black 5s' Nos 44973 and 44707 (complete with snowplough) make a fine sight standing at Fort William shed in 1960. Other LNER types, including 'K1' No 62011, are also seen behind No 44973 which seems to have been cleaned — but not her tender! *The late David Hepburne-Scott/Colour-Rail*

Right:
The turntable at Fort William has been preserved at Kidderminster on the Severn Valley Railway and operates to this day. 'Black 5' No 44975 is in attendance on shed in April 1962. A snowplough is seen behind the tender of the locomotive. A spotter or photographer seems to be making haste across the turntable — had he been spotted by the shed staff without a permit?! *SC331 Colour-Rail*

Above:
Another 'J36', No 65300, shunts wagons in Fort William yard in March 1959. Freight traffic was heavier on the West Highland than the Callander & Oban: as well as coal, fish, general merchandise and oils there was traffic to and from Fife and Blyth from the aluminium plant at Fort William, No 65300 having some of these wagons in the train. Wood pulp also passed through the yards to and from the paper mill at Corpach. *The late David Hepburne-Scott/Colour-Rail*

Right:
'K1' 2-6-0 No 62012 backs out of Fort William station towards the yard with a van after having arrived with the 5.52pm ex-Mallaig on 22 May 1961. The 'K1s' were introduced by A. H. Peppercorn in 1949, the design being taken from the 1937-built Gresley 'K4s' which were designed for the West Highland. *Mike Mensing*

Above:
Ex-LMS '4F' 0-6-0 No 44255 which was allocated to 65J (Fort William and Mallaig) is seen drawing wagons and a coach out of Fort William yard, which was situated by the shed. The locomotive has a roller-shutter cover to protect the crew from the ravages of winter — although it is 25 May 1961. *Mike Mensing*

Right:
0-6-0 350hp diesel shunter D4098 heads a short local freight from Corpach paper mill to Fort William yard. The development of the paper mill at Corpach helped the case for the retention of the West Highland routes and has generated much business for the railway. The train is crossing Loch viaduct on 16 July 1965. *Mike Mensing*

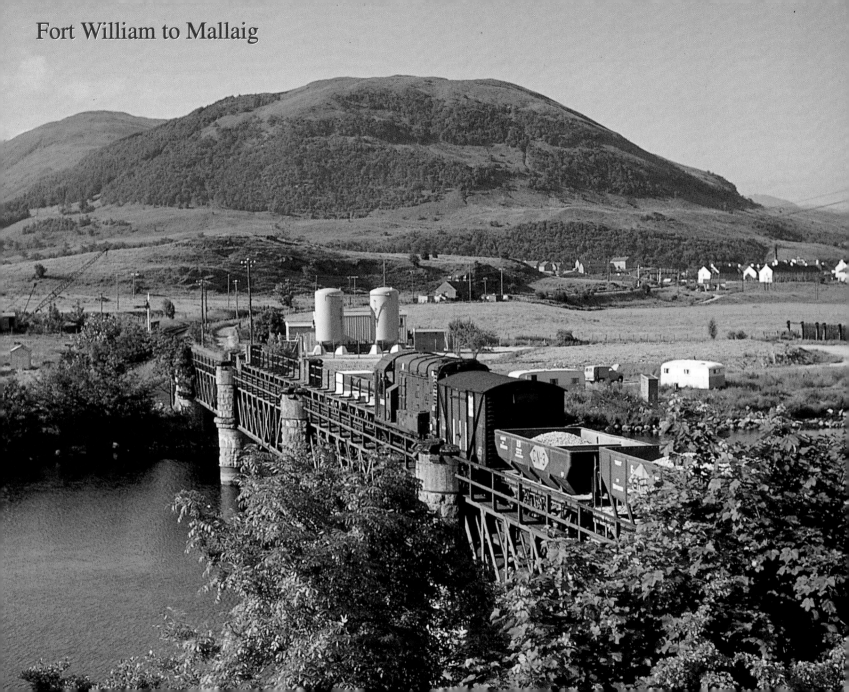

Left:
NBL Bo-Bo D6153 leaves Banavie with a service from Fort William to Mallaig in April 1968. Banavie Pier was once the terminus of a branch from Fort William to provide connections for steamers on the Caledonian Canal. The line closed to passengers in 1939 and to freight in 1951. At Banavie Junction the Mallaig extension began, which was just a single point and signalbox. By this time steam had gone and the new corporate blue/grey livery was replacing maroon on the coaching stock. Banavie station signalbox has now been replaced by a modern structure which controls the entire West Highland lines using Radio Electronic Token Block (RETB).
The late Derek Cross/Colour-Rail

Above:
'K2' 2-6-0 No 61764 heads a train for Mallaig near Corpach in July 1959. The 'K2s' were a Gresley GN design dating from 1914 of which the 'K2/2' variation, which had side windows in their cabs, operated in Scotland. West Highland 'K2s' were allocated to Eastfield shed (65A) which maintained Nos 61764, 61785-9, 61794, and to Fort William/Mallaig shed (65J) where Nos 61784 and 61791 were based.
SC512 Colour-Rail

Left:
NBL Bo-Bo D6129, carrying the then new 'corporate blue' livery, takes a train from Mallaig to Fort William past Locheilside in April 1968. However, this was in the era of mixed liveries and the coaching stock is still in maroon. The vehicle behind the locomotive is a Gresley full brake. The run from Mallaig Junction at Fort William is relatively level for the first 13 miles before a climb through Glenfinnan begins.
The late Derek Cross/Colour-Rail

Above:
A view from a Fort William-bound train near Glenfinnan on 9 May 1959 sees 'K2/2' No 61789 *Loch Laidon* about to enter a short tunnel. The construction engineers of the Mallaig extension, Robert McAlpine's, had hoped to get away with the construction of only two tunnels. In the end, 11 were needed. *Colour-Rail*

Right:
A view of the magnificent concrete viaduct at Glenfinnan is had from a double-headed traditional mixed train for Fort William and Glasgow with 'K1s' Nos 62034 and 62012 in charge on 24 July 1957. *Colour-Rail*

Left:
Heading in the opposite direction, 'K2' No 61784 passes over Glenfinnan viaduct with a Mallaig service on 9 May 1959. The viaduct is 1,248ft long, has 21 arches and was built out of concrete by the contractor Robert McAlpine and Sons. This viaduct has to be the most striking feature of the West Highland lines. *Colour-Rail*

Above:
A spectacular view of the Mallaig line scenery that sums up the remoteness of the line as it snakes towards the port. Two 'K2s', Nos 61791 and 61995, get away from Glenfinnan making for Mallaig with a traditional mixed train in March 1956. *SC738 Colour-Rail*

Left:
BRCW Bo-Bo D5349 passes Loch Eilt with the 10.5am Glasgow Queen Street to Mallaig on 6 July 1965. The last coach is SC1719E, an observation car converted from the LNER Coronation 'Beaver Tail' cars of 1937. These were modified by Cowlairs works specially for West Highland services, but of course they required turning and were shunted onto locomotive turntables for this purpose.
Mike Mensing

Above:
Another view of the train to Fort William, seen earlier at Glenfinnan, hauled by 'K1s' Nos 62034 and 62012 on 24 July 1957. The train is seen at Lochailort and is about to storm the 1:48 climb over Glenfinnan. This is a fine example of a mixed service which was so common on the Mallaig line. Lochailort was a crossing point which was lengthened in the war to allow for longer trains. The loop has since been removed.
Colour-Rail

Above:
Mallaig station is seen on 23 July 1957 with 'K1s' Nos 62052 and 62034 at the east end of the platforms. The 'K1' was introduced from 1949 and was a Peppercorn development of the Gresley 'K4' class that was designed specially for the West Highland services. One of the 'K4s' was rebuilt by Thompson in 1945 as a 'K1/1' — No 61997 *MacCallin Mor*. It had two outside cylinders instead of the 'K4s' three and was the forerunner of the Peppercorn locomotives which were longer. The 'K4s' were still more powerful than the 'K1s', having a tractive effort of 36,600lb instead of 32,080lb. Note the unusual signal, the NBR and LNER used latice posts. *Colour-Rail*

Right:
'K2' No 61789 *Loch Laidon* gets away from Mallaig with the 6.18pm to Fort William on 23 July 1957. The line towards Glenfinnan passed through Morar, Arisaig, Beasdale and Lochailort — a series of short banks and tight curves making for difficult and skilful handling of locomotives and trains. *Colour-Rail*

Railway colour books from IAN ALLAN Publishing

The Heyday of Steam in South Wales
By Derek Huntriss ISBN: 071102443X 7.25in x 9.5in H/B **£11.99**

The Heyday of Steam: West Midlands
By John B. Bucknall ISBN: 0711024502 7.25in x 9.5in H/B **£11.99**

The Heyday of Steam: Swindon & Its Locomotives
By R. C. Riley ISBN: 0711024820 7.25in x 9.5in H/B **£11.99**

On London & North Western Lines
By Derek Huntriss ISBN: 0711023824 7.25in x 9.5in H/B **£10.99**

On Somerset & Dorset Lines
By Robert Robotham ISBN: 0711024138 7.25in x 9.5in H/B **£10.99**

On The Waverley Route
By Robert Robotham ISBN: 0711024146 7.25in x 9.5in H/B **£10.99**

Railway Roundabout
By Rex Christiansen ISBN: 0711024561 11.5in x 8.5in H/B **£16.99**

Steam in Somerset
By Derek Huntriss ISBN: 0711024790 7.25in x 9.5in H/B **£11.99**